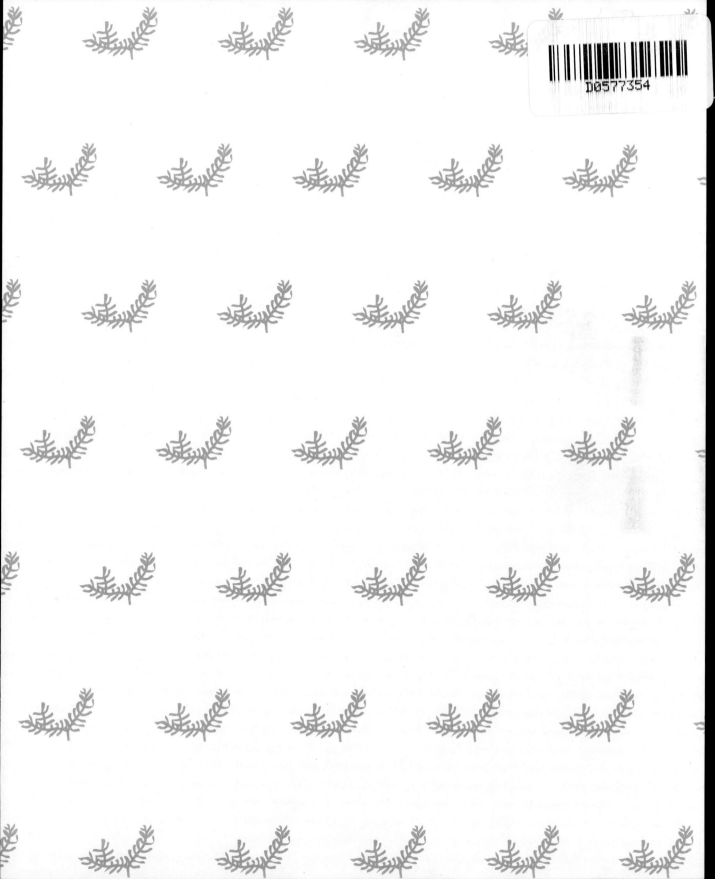

THE NEW PLANT LIBRARY

HEATHERS

THE NEW PLANT LIBRARY

HEATHERS

ANDREW MIKOLAJSKI

Consultant: David Small
Photography by Peter Anderson

LORENZ BOOKS
NEW YORK • LONDON • SYDNEY • BATH

Lorenz books is an imprint of
Anness Publishing Inc.
27 West 20th Street
New York, NY 10011

© Anness Publishing Limited 1997

ISBN 1 85967 514 X

Publisher: Joanna Lorenz
Senior Editor: Clare Nicholson
Designer: Michael Morey
Photographer: Peter Anderson

Printed in Hong Kong

3 5 7 9 10 8 6 4 2

Contents

INTRODUCTION

The history of heathers *8*

Heathers as garden plants *12*

The heather plant *18*

PLANT CATALOGUE

THE GROWER'S GUIDE

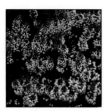

Buying heathers *40*

Cultivation of heathers *41*

Planting a heather bed *42*

Making a raised heather bed *44*

Growing heathers in containers *46*

Growing heathers in hanging baskets *48*

Routine maintenance *49*

Pruning heathers *50*

Propagation of heathers *52*

Heathers for indoor decoration *56*

Heather problems *58*

Calendar *59*

Other recommended heathers *60*

Index *63*

Introduction

*H*eathers are among the most enduring garden performers and are now enjoying a deserved renaissance. Tough and hardy, most can withstand extreme conditions, and some even put on their finest performance when the weather is at its most severe. One of the many advantages of heathers is that they enable us to enjoy continuous garden colour. Not only is there a heather in flower every month of the year, but some have coloured foliage that can itself be a strong, year-round feature, the leaf colour often changing with the seasons. This book shows you the many ways in which all heathers can be enjoyed, whether grown in island beds, raised beds (for gardeners who do not have acid soil) or containers, and describes and illustrates some of the many exciting cultivars available to the gardener today.

■ RIGHT
A display of heathers that enlivens a vista without in any way blocking it.

The history of heathers

Heathers are commonly held to comprise three genera: *Calluna*, *Daboecia* and *Erica*. Strictly speaking, the term "heather" applies only to *Calluna* (which also has the common name "ling", though this is virtually obsolete), "heath" being used for *Erica*. There is no widely used common name for *Daboecia*. In this book "heather" is used to cover all three. The related *Phyllodoce* are sometimes also referred to as heathers, but they are omitted from this book. The three genera belong to the family *Ericaceae*, and are broadly similar in appearance and cultivation needs.

Heathers are widespread throughout Europe and beyond. *Calluna* is found in western Europe from the Arctic circle to southern Spain and Morocco, extending to the Czech Republic and Turkey. It has naturalized in eastern Canada from packing material used by the early settlers but is otherwise absent from America, Australasia and most of Asia. *Daboecia* grows in Ireland, France,

Spain, Portugal and the Azores. *Erica* occurs throughout western Europe, in African countries bordering the Mediterranean Sea, East Africa and South Africa. The typical habitat for *Calluna* and *Daboecia* is open, windswept, acid moorland where the soil is usually poor and rainfall high. In such situations heathers colonize great tracts of land and are a spectacular sight in full flower. *Erica* has a variety of habitats, from wet moorland to dry heathland; some South African species have unique habitats.

Heathers are tough plants, often grazed by deer and sheep. In Scotland grouse feed on the tips of the shoots, and it is commonly believed that the meat owes some of its flavour to the heather. *Erica erigena* is particularly valued by bee-keepers since it is in flower, and a pollen source, between late winter and early spring when few other flowers are open.

Heather has been used as a medicinal plant to cure the common cold, urinary problems, arthritis and rheumatism. Heather honey is still widely supposed to improve health and, to this day, white heather symbolizes good luck.

In parts of Scotland and Ireland, where heathers predominate, peasant dwellings were traditionally built from clumps of heather. These were dug up to be used as bricks, the roots facing outwards, and the topgrowth plastered with a mix of mud and straw. Heather was also used to thatch roofs, and inside served as a fuel. Its common name "ling" derives from the Anglo-Saxon word *lig*, meaning fire.

Heather was additionally used for making brooms and scrubbing brushes, particularly in Greece. (The name *Calluna* derives from the Greek *kallunein*, meaning to cleanse, referring either to the use of heather twigs as brooms or to the medicinal properties of the plant.) *Erica arborea* (the Tree heath) was used to make briar pipes, the term "briar" being a corruption of the French word *bruyère*, meaning heather.

In 1776 the British government acknowledged the use of heath-tan, a heather extract, in the tanning of leather. A yellow die extracted by boiling the crushed shoots and stems was blended with other dies for colouring yarns and cloths. Heather beer is known to have been brewed on the Isle of Islay, other ingredients including barley malt and *Myrica gale* (the Bog myrtle). Heather beer is still

brewed today. The 19th-century poet Robert Louis Stevenson refers to an even more potent brew in *Heather Ale*, the Picts of Galloway preferring death by the invading Irish to yielding up the secrets of its manufacture.

Little is known of the history of heathers in gardens. The 17th-century herbalists do not refer to them, and before the 19th century they scarcely figured as important garden plants, though by the early 1800s there were 400 varieties in cultivation. (Today we have about 1,100.) Perhaps because they were so widespread in the wild, to say nothing of their associations with the peasant classes, they did not have the appeal of exotic imports from the East. It is difficult to imagine heathers being planted in the formalized gardens of Renaissance Italy or of Louis XIV's Versailles. However, when "Capability" Brown became the leading exponent of landscape gardening in 18th-century England, the lowly heather could at last play a role.

Around this time the vogue for all things Celtic swept across Europe, a phenomenon that lasted well into the 19th century. Gardeners began to

A richly planted rockery that brings
heathers into close contact with lush,
moisture-loving plants.

devote whole areas to acid-loving
plants, such as heathers and rhododendrons, combined with large
rockeries and moss and fern gardens,
the whole creating a jungle-like effect.
This so-called "wild" gardening grew
in popularity from the middle of the
19th century, fostered by the English
gardening writers William Robinson
and Shirley Hibberd, the idea being to
emulate nature as far as possible,
concentrating on hardy plants,
particularly natives and imported
plants that naturalized easily.

A new way of growing heathers was
developed from the middle of the 20th
century by Adrian Bloom, who
invented island beds. These are usually
roughly triangular, oval or kidney-
shaped, and are informally planted,
since they are designed to be viewed
from more than one side unlike the
rather theatrical, traditional herbaceous
border. Low-maintenance ground-
cover plants that effectively smother
weeds are vital in such a planting, and
heathers are the perfect choice. They
rapidly form impenetrable mats that
provide interest over a long season.

■ RIGHT
Adrian Bloom pioneered the island bed
planted with heathers and conifers that
allows views across the garden, into the
middle distance.

Heathers as garden plants

Heathers are usually best planted on their own in drifts, as they grow in the wild, knitting together to form mats of colour. By judicious selection among the genera they can provide year-round interest. Many *Erica* flower in the winter and spring, with *Calluna* taking over in summer and autumn. Some of each have forms with coloured foliage that are a strong feature all year long, though in some cases this will vary in intensity according to the season and local climate.

The colours of heathers are akin to those found in some once glorious, but now slightly faded, medieval tapestries. White, rich purples and dusky pinks are complemented by the old golds and warm orange-reds of the foliage varieties – none of them flashy individually but all striking in combination. Since they are generally low-growing, a carpet of flowers can be realized easily. For the maximum impact, group them by flowering season so that you have separate areas

■ RIGHT
One of the most outstanding heathers, *Erica carnea* 'Springwood White' is a spectacle from mid-winter onwards.

■ BELOW
Even in the depths of winter heathers are resilient performers, a riming of frost adding to their appeal.

PLANT COMBINATIONS

Acid-loving plants that associate well with heathers

Andromeda polifolia and cultivars

Arctostaphylos uva-ursi and cultivars

Cytisus scoparius

Gaultheria mucronata and cultivars

Pieris japonica and cultivars

Rhododendron impeditum

Rhododendron keiskei

Ulex europaeus

Vaccinium vitis-idaea

for summer and winter interest. Even when they are not in flower they will provide a dense, weed-suppressing mass that you can brighten up by incorporating cultivars with coloured foliage. Irregularly shaped beds look best. Avoid a spotty look by planting in groups of three, or more.

You can lift the eye by dotting about occasional accent plants. Try the Tree heath, though not where hard frosts are frequent, or an upright dwarf conifer such as the Irish juniper (*Juniperus communis* 'Hibernica') or *Thuja orientalis* 'Aurea Nana'.

Conifers and heathers are natural allies, both enjoying the same conditions, and you can create living, organic sculptures by combining them, all the plants gradually merging to form a compound, fluid structure. Remember, too, that though conifers provide year-round interest, the blue-leaved forms, such as *Juniperus squamata* 'Blue Star', will have their most intense colour after the first frosts, while the golden-leaved forms, such as *Thuja plicata* 'Stoneham Gold', are best in early spring.

An effective use of heathers, but

one that is seldom exploited, is as an edging plant to a shrub border. They can fulfil the same purpose in a relatively informal scheme as does tightly clipped box, lavender or *Santolina* in a formal one. The compact, upright *Calluna vulgaris* 'Cuprea' is a good choice, its distinctive, coppery-red foliage deepening to bronze-red in winter. Compact varieties of *Erica carnea* such as 'Vivellii' and 'Adrienne Duncan' are equally suitable.

■ RIGHT
Erica lusitanica makes an unusual hedge if closely clipped; the bare section will respond well to hard pruning.

Seasonal interest

Heathers are most highly rated as plants for the winter garden. Choose from varieties of *Erica carnea* and *E. × darleyensis*, perhaps mixing in selections of *Calluna vulgaris* with coloured foliage such as 'Beoley Gold' (bright golden yellow) or 'Robert Chapman' (gold, turning orange-red). Try some of the shrubs that have striking, colourful winter stems, such as the dogwoods (*Cornus*) and some willows (*Salix*), or plants that actually flower in winter, such as *Viburnum × bodnantense* 'Dawn', which has scented pink flowers. White-stemmed birches such as *Betula utilis* var. *jacquemontii* are among other possibilities. You could also brighten up your garden by including a few early bulbs, such as snowdrops (*Galanthus*), *Crocus chrysanthus* and *Iris reticulata*, so that the garden will be nearly as colourful as it is in summer, albeit in a softer range.

In summer, varieties of *Calluna vulgaris*, *Erica cinerea* and *E. vagans* dominate the scene, all effective with other acid-loving plants. To give height to a scheme, use either *Ulex europaeus* (gorse) or *Genista aetnensis* (Mount Etna Broom), both with fragrant, yellow, pea-like flowers.

A striking association can be formed by using a late-flowering clematis that flowers from mid- to late summer to meander through the heathers. The less vigorous *viticella* or *texensis* types of clematis, both with small flowers that are in the same colour range as the heathers, are best

■ ABOVE
As an edging to a shrub border, heathers provide a softer line than the more conventional *Buxus sempervirens.*

■ RIGHT
A sumptuous planting of heathers, conifers and other acid-loving plants, the spiky leaved yuccas in the foreground making an exotic accent.

Dwarf Conifers

Dwarf conifers to plant with heathers (all are suitable, the following being particularly recommended)

Abies concolor 'Compacta'

Abies lasiocarpa var. *arizonica* 'Compacta'

Chamaecyparis pisifera 'Filifera Aurea'

Chamaecyparis obtusa 'Nana Aurea'

Juniperus communis 'Hibernica'

Juniperus procumbens 'Nana'

Juniperus squamata 'Blue Star'

Juniperus squamata 'Holger'

Juniperus virginiana 'Grey Owl'

Juniperus × *media* 'Pfitzeriana'

Juniperus × *media* 'Plumosa Aurea'

Microbiota decussata

Picea glauca var. *albertiana* 'Conica'

Picea mariana 'Nana'

Pinus heldreichii var. *leucodermis* 'Schmidtii'

Thuja orientalis 'Aurea Nana'

Thuja plicata 'Stoneham Gold'

■ LEFT
Island beds densely planted for a tapestry-like effect.

■ ABOVE
A drift of *Erica* × *darleyensis* 'Margaret Porter' glows in the winter sun.

■ BELOW
Heathers are the star performers at the quiet times of year, inviting you to venture into the garden even on the darkest days.

for this purpose. The summer-flowering species would be too rampant and would choke the heathers. The flowers of *Clematis* 'Royal Velours' would glow like rubies among the velvety old gold foliage of *Erica carnea* 'Foxhollow', for instance. If you site a clematis among winter-flowering *Erica*, however, you will have to cut it back in late autumn rather than late winter, as is generally recommended, since the heathers need to enjoy their season of glory without the covering of dead clematis stems. The clematis will come to no harm since the heathers themselves will protect any precocious new shoots from the clematis.

HEATHERS GROWN FOR THEIR COLOURED FOLIAGE
(UNLESS OTHERWISE INDICATED, COLOUR CHANGES OCCUR IN WINTER)

Calluna vulgaris
'Beoley Gold' (golden-yellow)
'Golden Feather' (gold, turning orange-red)
'Multicolor' (yellowish-green, tipped with orange and coral-red)
'Red Carpet' (gold, turning orange-red)
'Red Fred' (dark green with vivid red tips in spring)
'Robert Chapman' (gold, turning orange-red)
'Roland Haagen' (gold, turning orange-red)
'Serlei Aurea' (yellowish-green, tipped bright yellow in spring and autumn)
'Sir John Charrington' (gold, turning orange-red)
'Sister Anne' (grey-green, turning bronze)
'Spring Cream' (cream tips on new growth)
'Sunset' (golden-yellow in spring, orange in autumn, red in winter)
'Wickwar Flame' (gold, turning orange-red)

Erica
E. carnea 'Ann Sparkes' (dark golden-yellow with bronze tips on new growth)
'Barry Sellers' (yellow, turning orange)
'Foxhollow' (yellow, turning slightly orange)
'Golden Starlet' (lime green, yellow in summer)
'Westwood Yellow' (yellow)
E. cinerea 'Fiddler's Gold' (golden-yellow, turning red)
'Golden Hue' (pale yellow, developing orange tips in winter)
'Lime Soda' (lime green)
'Rock Pool' (golden-yellow, turning orange-red)
'Windlebrooke' (golden-yellow, turning orange-red)
E. × darleyensis 'Jenny Porter' (cream tips on new growth)
'J.W. Porter' (red and cream tips on new growth)
E. erigena 'Golden Lady' (golden-yellow)
E. vagans 'Valerie Proudley' (bright yellow)

The heather plant

Heathers are tough, usually hardy, evergreen sub-shrubs or shrubs, and most form hummocks up to 90cm (3ft) high. Though they are usually upright growing, seen *en masse* (when growing in the wild) they merge to form a carpet. Many dwarf forms are much smaller, but there are also some taller heathers, as described below.

Heathers produce bell- or urn-shaped flowers. *Calluna* has small, scale-like leaves that are closely pressed together. *Erica* has needle-like leaves, and those of *Daboecia* are slightly broader, tending towards a lance shape.

There is only one species of *Calluna*, *C. vulgaris*, but it has more than 500 cultivars, all suitable as ground cover. The flowers are bell-shaped and are carried on short stalks attached to a main stem, the whole structure known as a raceme.

Daboecia has two species, the half-hardy *D. azorica* and the hardy *D. cantabrica,* which has many cultivars. The two species have hybridized to produce the hardy *D. × scotica,* which also has many fine cultivars. *Daboecia* is distinguished from *Calluna* by having urn-shaped flowers, also carried in racemes. They tend to be larger than those of the other two genera.

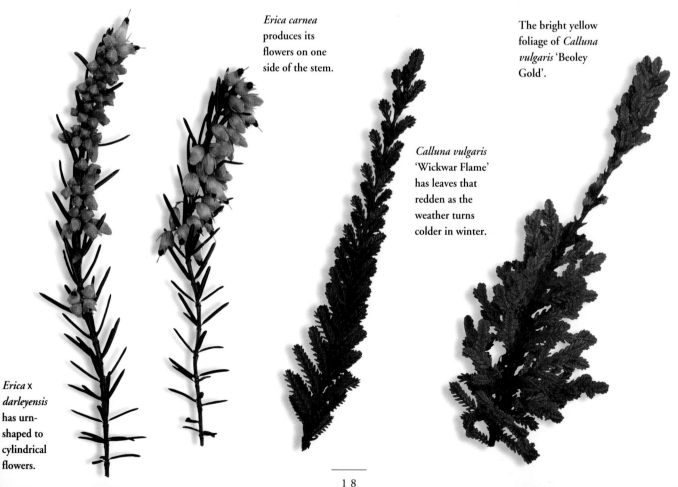

Erica carnea produces its flowers on one side of the stem.

The bright yellow foliage of *Calluna vulgaris* 'Beoley Gold'.

Calluna vulgaris 'Wickwar Flame' has leaves that redden as the weather turns colder in winter.

Erica x *darleyensis* has urn-shaped to cylindrical flowers.

Erica is the largest genus, with 700 or more species, but only around thirty to forty are widely grown in gardens. The most important are *E. carnea* and *E. cinerea*, both of which have many cultivars. Other important members of the genus are *E. mackaiana*, *E. vagans* and the hybrids *E. × darleyensis*, *E. × stuartii* and *E. × williamsii*.

Erica has bell or urn-shaped flowers that are distinguished from those of *Calluna* by having prominent corollas (the petals of the flower) and usually green calyces (the structure that encloses the bud). They are carried in racemes, umbels (on stalks from a single point at the top of the stem), clusters (like umbels but along the stem) or panicles (branched racemes).

Erica includes some larger heathers, such as the tree-like *E. arborea* (The Tree heath) that can reach a height of 6m (20ft) and the smaller *E. australis,* which grows to 2m (6ft). Both make fine specimen plants, though neither is reliably hardy in cold districts. The South African *E. canaliculata,* which also reaches a height of 2m (6ft), is for frost-free gardens only.

Calluna vulgaris 'Darkness' has rich dark green foliage and crimson flowers.

The foliage of *Calluna vulgaris* deepens in colour in winter. Many heathers change foliage through the seasons.

A stem of the upright-growing *Erica arborea* var. *alpina.*

Calluna vulgaris

In this section, heathers are arranged alphabetically by botanical name. Heights and spreads are what the plants can be expected to achieve after three years given good growing conditions and will vary according to soil type, climate and season. All the heathers described here are hardy to –15°C (5°F) apart from *Erica lusitanica*, which does not generally tolerate a temperature lower than –5°C (23°F).

■ ABOVE
'ALBA RIGIDA'

Heather with racemes of bell-shaped, white flowers from mid-summer to late autumn. Height 15cm (6in) spread 30cm (12in). *Calluna vulgaris* 'Alba Rigida' has a close and distinctive habit.

■ RIGHT
'ALISON YATES'

Heather with long racemes of white flowers from mid-summer to late autumn and silver-grey leaves. Height 45cm (18in), spread 60cm (24in). *Calluna vulgaris* 'Alison Yates' is a vigorous plant.

■ ABOVE
'DARK BEAUTY'

Heather with racemes of semi-double blood red flowers from mid-summer to late autumn and dark green foliage. Height 25cm (10in), spread 35cm (14in).

■ ABOVE LEFT
'ARRAN GOLD'

Heather with racemes of purple flowers from mid-summer to late autumn and bright golden yellow foliage that is lime-green flecked with red in winter. Height 15cm (6in), spread 25cm (10in).

■ LEFT
'DARKNESS'

Heather with short racemes of bright crimson flowers from mid-summer to late autumn and dark green foliage. Height 25cm (10in), spread 35cm (14in). *Calluna vulgaris* 'Darkness' is a compact, upright plant.

■ ABOVE

'FIREFLY'

Heather with short racemes of pinkish-lilac flowers from mid-summer to late autumn; the foliage is warm orange-red in summer, darkening to brick red in winter. Height 45cm (18in), spread 50cm (20in).

■ LEFT

'HAMMONDII AUREIFOLIA'

Heather with short racemes of white flowers from mid-summer to late autumn; the mid-green foliage is tipped yellow in spring. Height 30cm (12in), spread 40cm (16in).

■ LEFT
'MY DREAM'

(syn. *C.v.* 'Snowball') Heather with long racemes of double white flowers from mid-summer to late autumn. Height 45cm (18in), spread to 75cm (30in). One of the most striking cultivars, *Calluna vulgaris* 'My Dream' is also good as a cut flower.

■ BELOW
'WICKWAR FLAME'

Heather with yellow to flame-orange foliage that deepens to brilliant orange-red in winter; the racemes of mauve-pink flowers, produced from mid-summer to late autumn, are best removed. Height 50cm (20in), spread 60cm (24in).

■ ABOVE
'TIB'

Heather with racemes of small, double, cyclamen purple flowers in early summer and dark green leaves. Height 30cm (12in), spread 40cm (16in). A vigorous plant, *Calluna vulgaris* 'Tib' is the earliest double cultivar to flower.

Daboecia cantabrica

■ RIGHT
'ALBA'

Heather with racemes of urn-shaped, white flowers from early summer to mid-autumn. Height 40cm (16in), spread 70cm (28in). Plants sold under this name may vary.

■ BELOW
'ATROPURPUREA'

Heather with urn-shaped, rich dark pinkish-purple flowers from early summer to mid-autumn; the foliage is bronze-tinted. Height 40cm (16in), spread 70cm (28in).

■ LEFT
'WALEY'S
RED'

(syn. *D.c.*
'Whalley')
Heather with
urn-shaped, deep
magenta flowers
from early
summer to mid-
autumn. Height
35cm (14in),
spread 50cm
(20in).

Erica australis

■ RIGHT
'RIVERSLEA'

Heather with tubular or bell-shaped,
lilac-pink flowers from mid- to late
spring. Height 1.2m (4ft), spread 85cm
(34in). More compact than the species,
Erica australis 'Riverslea' is an
outstanding tree heath.

Erica carnea

■ LEFT
'AUREA'

Heather with urn-shaped flowers in late winter and early spring that open pink and age darker; the foliage, gold all year, is tipped with orange in spring. Height 15cm (6in), spread 35cm (14in). *Erica carnea* 'Aurea' is a neat, compact plant.

■ BELOW
'EILEEN PORTER'

Heather with urn-shaped flowers with magenta corollas and cream sepals from autumn to early spring. Height and spread 20cm (8in). *Erica carnea* 'Eileen Porter' is a slow-growing heather.

■ RIGHT
'KING GEORGE'

Heather with urn-shaped, pink flowers, darkening with age, from late winter to early spring and dark green foliage. Height 15cm (6in), spread 25cm (10in). 'King George' is one of the most compact cultivars of *Erica carnea*.

■ LEFT
'MYRETOUN RUBY'

Heather with urn-shaped, pink flowers that turn to magenta then crimson from late winter to early spring and dark green foliage. Height 15cm (6in), spread 45 cm (18in). *Erica carnea* 'Myretoun Ruby' is considered one of the best winter-flowering heathers in its colour range.

■ LEFT
'PRAECOX RUBRA'

Heather with urn-shaped, lilac-pink flowers from early winter to spring; the foliage is sometimes tinged with brown. Height 15cm (6in), spread 40cm (16in). *Erica carnea* 'Praecox Rubra' is a vigorous plant with a semi-prostrate habit.

■ RIGHT

'SPRINGWOOD WHITE'

Heather with masses of urn-shaped, white flowers from late winter to mid-spring. Height 15cm (6in), spread 45cm (18in). *Erica carnea* 'Springwood White' is a vigorous, trailing cultivar; its long and generous flowering makes it one of the most outstanding winter heathers.

■ BELOW

'ROSY GEM'

Heather with urn-shaped, lilac-pink flowers from mid-winter to spring; the foliage is dark green. Height 20cm (8in), spread 45cm (18in).

■ BELOW

'VIVELLII'

(syn. *E.c.* 'Urville') Heather with urn-shaped, lilac-pink flowers that deepen to magenta from late winter to early spring; the dark green foliage is tinged bronze. Height 15cm (6in), spread 35cm (14in).

Erica cinerea

■ LEFT
'ALFRED BOWERMAN'

Heather with urn-shaped, brick-red or dusky pink flowers from early summer to early autumn. Height 35cm (14in), spread 45cm (18in). *Erica cinerea* 'Alfred Bowerman' is a vigorous plant of upright habit.

■ BELOW
'C.D. EASON'

Heather with urn-shaped, glowing, bright magenta-pink flowers from early summer to early autumn offset by dark, dull green leaves. Height 25cm (10in), spread 50cm (20in). A bushy plant, *Erica cinerea* 'C.D. Eason' makes excellent ground cover.

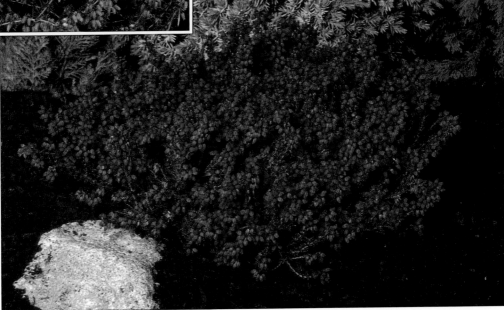

■ LEFT

'C.G. BEST'

Heather with long spikes of urn-shaped, salmon-pink flowers from early summer to early autumn. Height 30cm (12in), spread 70cm (28in). *Erica cinerea* 'C.G. Best' is a graceful plant.

■ ABOVE

'FIDDLER'S GOLD'

Heather with urn-shaped, lilac-pink flowers from early summer to early autumn and bright golden-yellow foliage that turns red in winter. Height 25cm (10in), spread 45cm (18in). *Erica cinerea* 'Fiddler's Gold' produces its best leaf colour in spring.

■ LEFT

'GOLDEN DROP'

Heather with bright golden-yellow foliage that is tinged copper on emergence in spring and turns copper-red in winter. The sparse, urn-shaped, lilac-pink flowers, produced from early summer to early autumn, are best removed. Height 20cm (8in), spread 60cm (24in). *Erica cinerea* 'Golden Drop' has a prostrate, mat-like habit that is good for ground cover.

■ LEFT
'GOLDEN SPORT'

Heather with urn-shaped, deep carmine-pink flowers from early summer to early autumn and bright golden-yellow leaves. Height 15cm (6in), spread 30cm (12in). *Erica cinerea* 'Golden Sport' produces its best foliage colour with regular pruning.

■ ABOVE
'HEIDEBRAND'

Heather with urn-shaped, bright flaming pink flowers from early summer to early autumn. Height 20cm (8in), spread 30cm (12in).

■ LEFT
'P.S. PATRICK'

Heather with urn-shaped, bright reddish-purple flowers from early summer to early autumn; the foliage is dark, glossy green, the shoots tipped with purplish-red. Height 30cm (12in), spread 45cm (18in). *Erica cinerea* 'P.S. Patrick' is one of the best in its colour range.

■ OPPOSITE

'PENTREATH'

Compact heather with urn-shaped, rich purple flowers from early summer to early autumn. Height 30cm (12in), spread 55cm (22in).

■ ABOVE

'SUMMER GOLD'

Heather with urn-shaped, magenta-pink flowers from early summer to early autumn and bright golden-yellow leaves. Height 30cm (12in), spread 45cm (18in). *Erica cinerea* 'Summer Gold' has an upright habit.

Erica × *darleyensis*

'ARCHIE GRAHAM'

Heather with urn-shaped to cylindrical flowers with lilac-pink sepals and pink corollas that deepen to lilac-pink from mid-winter to early spring. Height 50cm (20in), spread 60cm (24in).

'ARTHUR JOHNSON'

(syn. *E.* × *darleyensis* 'A.T. Johnson') Heather with urn-shaped to cylindrical, pink flowers that deepen to lilac-pink from mid-winter to early spring; the foliage is tipped with cream in spring. Height 60cm (24in), spread 75cm (30in).

'JACK H. BRUMMAGE'

(syn. *E.* × *darleyensis* 'J. H. Brummage', *E. erigena* 'Jack H. Brummage') Heather with urn-shaped to cylindrical, lilac-pink flowers from mid-winter to late spring; the foliage is yellow-orange throughout the year. Height 30cm (12in), spread 60cm (24in).

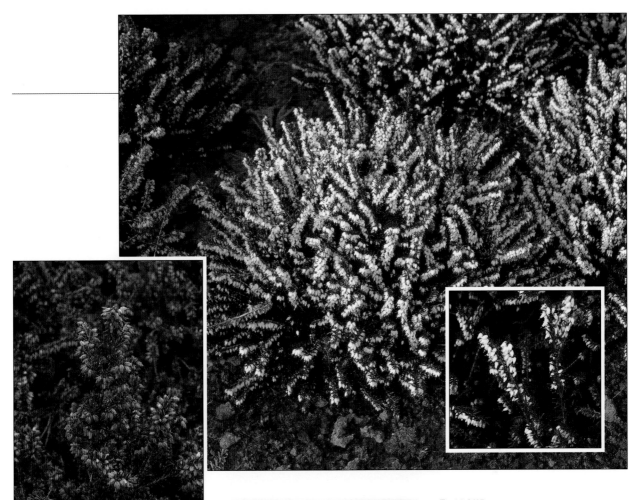

■ ABOVE
'KRAMERS RÖTE'

(syn. *E.* × *darleyensis* 'Kramer's Red')
Heather with urn-shaped to cylindrical,
magenta flowers from mid-winter to
spring; the foliage is tinged bronze.
Height 35cm (14in), spread 60cm
(24in). An outstanding introduction,
Erica × *darleyensis* 'Kramers Röte'
combines the flower colour of *E. carnea*
'Myretoun Ruby' (one of its parents)
with attractively coloured foliage.

■ ABOVE
'SILBERSCHMELZE'

(syn. *E.* × *darleyensis* 'Molten Silver',
'Silver Beads') Heather with urn-shaped
to cylindrical, ash-white flowers from
mid-winter to late spring; the foliage is
faintly tipped with cream in spring.
Height 35cm (14in), spread 80cm (32in).

■ LEFT
'WHITE PERFECTION'

Heather with urn-shaped to cylindrical,
pure white flowers from mid-winter to
spring. Height 40cm (16in), spread
70cm (28in). *Erica* × *darleyensis* 'White
Perfection' is one of the best white
heathers.

Erica erigena

■ ABOVE
'BRIAN PROUDLEY'

Heather with long racemes of urn-shaped to cylindrical, white flowers from early to mid-spring. Height 90cm (3ft), spread 40cm (16in). An outstanding introduction, *Erica erigena* 'Brian Proudley' is vigorous and free-flowering.

Erica lusitanica

■ RIGHT
'GEORGE HUNT'

Erect heather with tubular to bell-shaped, white flowers in spring; the feathery foliage is bright yellow throughout the year. Height 70cm (40in), spread 45cm (18in). Outstanding as a specimen plant and more compact than the species, *Erica lusitanica* 'George Hunt' needs a sheltered site.

Erica manipuliflora ssp. anthura

■ LEFT
'HEAVEN
SCENT'

Heather with
fragrant,
cylindrical to
bell-shaped, lilac-
pink flowers in
late summer and
autumn. Height
to 90cm (3ft),
spread to 60cm
(2ft). *Erica
manipuliflora* ssp.
anthura 'Heaven
Scent' is a
vigorous plant of
upright habit.

Erica × stuartii

■ RIGHT
'IRISH LEMON'

(syn. *E. erigena* 'Irish Lemon', *E. hybrida* 'Irish Lemon')
Heather with large, urn-shaped, mauve flowers from late spring
to early autumn; the new growth in spring is bright lemon
yellow. Height 25cm (10in), spread 50cm (20in). 'Irish Lemon'
and other selections of *Erica × stuartii* need moist soil.

Erica vagans

■ BELOW
'BIRCH GLOW'

Heather with cylindrical to bell-shaped, glowing rose-pink flowers from mid-summer to mid-autumn and bright green leaves. Height 30cm (12in), spread 50cm (20in).

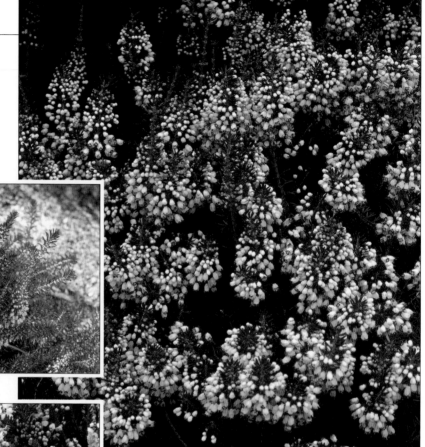

■ ABOVE
'HOOKSTONE ROSEA'

Heather with cylindrical to bell-shaped, pale rose-pink flowers from mid-summer to mid-autumn. Height 35cm (14in), spread 70cm (28in).

■ LEFT
'SUMMERTIME'

Heather with cylindrical to bell-shaped, pretty shell-pink flowers from mid-summer to mid-autumn. Height 15cm (6in), spread 35cm (14in). *Erica vagans* 'Summertime' is a neat, compact plant.

■ RIGHT
'VALERIE PROUDLEY'

Heather with cylindrical to bell-shaped, sparse, white flowers from mid-summer to mid-autumn and bright lemon-yellow leaves. Height 15cm (6in), spread 30cm (12in). The foliage of *Erica vagans* 'Valerie Proudley' is of good colour throughout the year; a good heather for a container.

■ RIGHT
'VIRIDIFLORA'

Heather that produces green bracts (modified leaves at the base of a flower) that are more conspicuous than the small, bluish-green or mauve flowers. Height 30cm (12in), spread 55cm (22in). *Erica vagans* 'Viridiflora' is good in flower arrangements.

Erica × williamsii

■ RIGHT
'P.D. WILLIAMS'

Heather with lilac-pink flowers from mid-summer to late autumn. The new growth is tipped bright yellow, the colour persisting until well into summer. Height 25cm (10in), spread 45cm (18in).

Buying heathers

Heathers are sold as container-grown plants in garden centres and by mail order, usually in 8–9cm (3–3½in) or 1 litre pots. Large plants are sometimes available at a higher price. Many large garden centres prefer to sell plants that are in flower, so not all species and their varieties are likely to be available at any one time. Heathers

are remarkably cheap, compared with most other plants, reflecting their ease of propagation, their low demand on fertilizers and their compactness.

Look for young, healthy plants that show no signs of disease. Check the root system by sliding the plant from its container. If the roots are tightly coiled round the pot the plant is pot-

bound and will be slow to establish.

Nurseries that specialize in heathers also often sell them as rooted cuttings in modules. Check with the supplier how long they have been rooted. If only recently rooted, pot them up and grow them on for the first season before planting them out. If they are well-rooted, however, it is safe to plant them out directly from the module, provided the site has been well prepared and the soil is friable.

■ ABOVE AND LEFT
Heathers are usually sold in 8–9cm (3–3½in) or 1 litre pots.

■ LEFT
When buying a plant, always have a look at the root ball to check it is not pot-bound.

Cultivation of heathers

Heathers need an open, sunny site. It is commonly assumed that they will grow only in acid soil, but this is true only of *Calluna* and some *Erica*. *Daboecia* will grow in neutral soil, while *Erica carnea*, *E.* × *darleyensis*, *E. erigena*, *E. manipuliflora*, *E. terminalis*, *E. vagans* and *E.* × *williamsii* tolerate alkaline soil. The ideal soil is light, friable, sandy and well-drained. Heathers do not need a very fertile soil.

All soils can be improved by digging in organic matter prior to planting. This opens up the texture of heavy soils and makes light soils more moisture retentive. If you have a very heavy clay soil that is prone to waterlogging, lighten it further by digging in coarse grit, about a bucketful per sq yd (sq m). If the water table is high you may need to lay a system of land drains for the heathers to thrive; alternatively, grow the heathers in a raised bed.

Soil acidity is expressed in terms of the pH scale, which runs from 1 to 14, 7 indicating neutral, the lower numbers acid, the higher alkaline. A pH of around 5–5.5 is ideal for most heathers. If you do not know whether your soil is acid or alkaline, you need to test it. Use either an electronic pH meter or, more cheaply, a soil testing kit. Both are available in most garden centres. Test the soil in more than one area since there can be pockets of alkaline soil in otherwise acid sites, and vice versa. The soil test involves mixing slowly dried soil with a chemical compound. The resulting colour indicates the degree of acidity or alkalinity. The meter gives an instant reading but is less accurate.

If you do not have acid soil, you can grow heather in containers or make a raised bed. There are some heathers that tolerate alkaline soil.

TESTING YOUR SOIL WITH A SOIL TESTING KIT

1 Take a small sample of soil from your garden, from 5–7.5cm (2–3in) below the soil surface, for the most representative reading.

2 Allow the sample to dry out slowly, then place it in the test tube and add water as recommended by the manufacturer.

3 Shake the test tube and wait for the contents to settle. Check the colour against the colour chart, indicating the acidity of your soil. Yellow or orange indicates acid soil, bright green neutral, and dark green alkaline soil.

Planting a heather bed

Heathers can be planted at any time of the year except during periods of summer drought or when the ground is frozen or waterlogged. For the best results plant in multiples of each variety. An odd number usually works best, and remember that too many different colours in proximity can look spotty.

Check the final spread of the plant to calculate how many you need to fill a given area. As a rough guide, for plants that have a spread of 15–30cm (6–12in), you will need five to fill 1sq m (1 sq yd). If you are in doubt, over- rather than underplant. You can always adjust the spacing and remove the surplus plants as they grow. It will be harder to plug gaps later when the plants have established and meshed together.

PLANTING HEATHERS

1 Clear the site of weeds and fork in organic matter (farmyard manure or garden compost) to improve the soil.

2 Set out the plants to determine their planting positions.

3 Dig holes with a trowel that will comfortably accommodate the rootballs. Heathers need to be planted deep enough so that the lower leaves are touching the soil.

4 Slide the plants from their containers and loosen the roots around the edge of the rootball with a hand fork.

5 Plant the heathers, backfill with the excavated soil, and firm them in with your fingers.

6 Water the heathers in well, then mulch with grit or bark chippings to retain moisture.

CULTIVATION UNDER GLASS

The genus *Erica* includes many tender species, most from South Africa, that cannot be grown successfully outdoors in cold climates, but that grow well under glass. *E. canaliculata* (flowering in late winter) and *E. gracilis* (late autumn) are the two most popular.

Tender heathers should be potted in a mixture of two parts ericaceous compost (soil mix) to one part horticultural sharp sand, preferably in terracotta pots, which are less likely to become waterlogged than plastic ones. Stand them in full light with good ventilation. When the plants are in active growth water them freely, ideally with rainwater, and apply a liquid tomato fertilizer at half strength every month. In summer, when temperatures under glass can soar, stand the plants outside. In winter, ensure that the plants remain frost free and that they have good ventilation. Keep the compost (soil mix) barely moist.

The compact *E. gracilis* and the hybrid *E. × hyemalis* are often sold as flowering houseplants in autumn and winter. (The latter is of uncertain parentage, and the name is loosely applied to various complex hybrids produced in the nursery trade.) They should be potted on immediately after purchase and kept well watered (over the foliage) in a cool place.

■ LEFT
After two or three years heathers will grow into each other to form a weed-suppressing carpet.

Making a raised heather bed

If your soil is alkaline you can still enjoy acid-loving heathers by growing them in raised beds. If your garden is on several levels, site the raised bed on a higher rather than a lower level. This prevents limy water from leaching down through the soil into the raised bed. Such beds are also unlikely to be successful where there is a high water table that creates boggy soil.

The bed should have a minimum depth of 23cm (9in), preferably more. You can fill it with ericaceous compost (soil mix), mixing it with leaf mould or garden compost where available, or you can buy in acid soil. Building contractors can often supply it; check

the gardening press for advertisements. However, if acid soil is unavailable within an 80km (50 mile) radius it is unlikely to be a viable option owing to high transportation costs.

Permanent raised beds are best made of brick, though it is expensive and labour-intensive. The work is best left to an experienced bricklayer. Furthermore, since mortar is limy, you will need to paint the interior with bituminous paint to prevent the lime from leaching into your soil. While brick is ideal for a town garden, it could look uncompromisingly hard in a rural one. Try speeding up the weathering effect by painting the

outside with sour milk or yoghurt to encourage the growth of moss and lichens. Stone is a good alternative to brick, but is even more expensive. Otherwise try railway sleepers (railroad ties). Since they are very heavy they do not need foundations, but do not lay them more than three sleepers (ties) high, as they do not easily bond together. A third option is to use log edging. This is available in flexible strips that can be used for round, oval or kidney-shaped beds or in rigid sections for geometric shapes.

Once the construction work is finished, sprinkle on flowers of sulphur (sulfur) at the base of the bed

MAKING A RAISED BED WITH A LOG EDGING

1 Set the log edging in position and tap it into place. Check the level with a spirit level. If you are using the flexible edging, drive in stakes to which you nail the edging.

2 On geometric shapes, as shown here, nail the corners together. Use rust-proof nails.

3 Fork over flowers of sulphur (sulfur), to reduce alkalinity, at the base of the bed at the recommended rate.

at the rate of 125gr per sq m (4oz per sq yd) for every point on the pH scale you wish the alkalinity to drop. The rate can be reduced to half that for sandy soils. The application takes six months to take effect. Then fill the bed with acid soil (or ericaceous compost), and plant it up (see Planting a heather bed). An annual topdressing of flowers of sulphur (sulfur) and ericaceous compost (soil mix) will keep the bed reasonably acidic indefinitely.

The important point about a raised bed is that it is, in effect, a huge container. It will need watering regularly during the growing season to prevent the soil from drying out.

■ ABOVE
A lively overspill of heathers in a small raised bed.

4 Six months later, fill the bed with acid soil – either soil imported from another source or ericaceous compost (soil mix).

5 Plant up the bed, water the plants in well, and mulch with shredded bark to retain moisture.

As an alternative to a raised bed make a mound out of the existing soil to a minimum depth of 23cm (9in). Fork in flowers of sulphur (sulfur) across the top at the recommended rate. Plant the sides (that will tend to remain fairly alkaline) with alkaline-tolerant heathers. These will grow into each other, forming a kind of thatch that will hold the bed together. Once the flowers of sulphur have taken effect, plant the top surface of the bed with acid-loving types. An island bed planted in this way makes an

Growing heathers in containers

Heathers are ideal subjects for containers and can be used to brighten up the terrace or patio in the depths of winter. Choose from dwarf, compact heathers such as *Calluna vulgaris* 'Golden Carpet' or 'Tib', or *Erica carnea* 'January Sun' or 'Ice Princess'. *Calluna vulgaris* has a number of cultivars, such as 'Anette' (pink), 'Alexandra' (red) and 'Alicia' (white), whose flowers fail to open fully and persist as buds from late summer to mid-winter, because they have not been fertilized. With their long season of interest, these are particularly valued for winter containers, hanging baskets and window boxes.

Combine heathers with dwarf conifers or dwarf rhododendrons to create a miniature garden. Winter-flowering pansies and miniature ivies could also be incorporated, as could some dwarf bulbs, to extend the season of interest. The dwarf irises *Iris danfordiae* (yellow) and *I. reticulata* (deep blue) are prime candidates, as are some daffodil species (eg. *Narcissus bulbocodium*). Scillas, chionodoxas and varieties of *Crocus chrysanthus* provide extra possibilities.

Deep containers are the most labour-saving since they will dry out less quickly. Terracotta, stone or wooden half barrels are ideal, as they are porous and unlikely to become seriously waterlogged. Glazed ceramic and plastic are less suitable, because they tend to retain moisture, and stay too moist for the heathers. Also try window boxes and hanging baskets.

Always use ericaceous compost (soil mix). You can replace up to half of it with garden compost or leaf mould. Top-dressing with grit after planting helps prevent excessive evaporation from the compost (soil mix) surface, while looking attractive in its own right.

Once planted, position the container in an open, sunny spot. Feeding throughout the growing season is not necessary, but a top-dressing in spring with blood,

PLANTING A CONTAINER FOR WINTER INTEREST

1 Choose a container made of a porous material such as terracotta, stone or wood. Cover the base with stones or crocks for efficient drainage.

2 Fill up the container to about one quarter of its depth with horticultural grit, again for improved drainage.

3 Begin to fill with ericaceous compost (soil mix).

■ LEFT
Once heathers have settled in they do not need much attention, and make an attractive present.

4 Decide on the best arrangement for the plants. Stand them on the compost (soil mix) surface. There should be a gap of about 2.5cm (1in) between the tops of their rootballs and the rim of the large container to allow for watering. If you are planting the container in the autumn or early winter, you could also add a few dwarf bulbs now.

■ LEFT
An elegant mix of heathers, *Skimmia*, *Cotoneaster horizontalis*, periwinkle and dwarf bamboos create a lively focal point.

5 Remove the heathers from their pots and set them in position. Here, dwarf conifers, winter-flowering pansies and miniature ivies were used. Water well using a can with a fine rose to avoid compacting the compost (soil mix), then top-dress with grit to ensure that the compost (soil mix) does not dry out.

fish and bone and an application of sequestered iron (iron chelate) are beneficial. Regular watering is necessary during the growing season.

Once the top 2.5cm (1in) of compost (soil mix) has dried out (test with your finger inserted at the edge of the container) water thoroughly. It is best to use rainwater. If only tapwater is available then the plants should be fed with half-strength tomato fertilizer plus sequestered iron. Domestically softened water should never be used.

With good maintenance the container will give pleasure over a

long period. If the heathers become straggly, replace them with younger specimens. When the other plants become too large, remove them and plant them out in the garden. Container plants are more vulnerable to freezing weather than plants in the open garden, since the roots are above ground level. To protect the plants during bad weather cover them loosely with dry straw or bracken, holding this in place with wire netting. Pack the plants loosely to permit good air circulation otherwise moisture may build up around the plants and freeze, killing them.

Growing heathers in hanging baskets

Heathers look good in hanging baskets, particularly in winter when they come into their own. They can create a basket that will give pleasure even in the darkest months.

Choose heathers that flower or have their best foliage in winter. Try mixing them with dwarf and prostrate conifers, winter-flowering pansies, and miniature ivies. Note, however, that heathers in hanging baskets are more susceptible to frost than plants in large containers kept on the ground. To prevent the roots from freezing during severe cold weather it is best to bring the baskets under cover, either into a porch or a cool greenhouse; even a carport provides adequate protection.

When planting, improve the drainage and prevent waterlogging by adding perlite to the compost (soil mix) instead of the horticultural grit recommended for containers. Grit would make the basket excessively heavy, difficult to lift, and a potential danger if strong winds bring it down. Water only to prevent the basket from drying out. As the plants begin to flag towards the end of winter, plant them out in the garden, or pot them up in fresh compost (soil mix).

PLANTING A HANGING BASKET

1 Position the basket on a flat surface. Large baskets can be worked more securely if placed over a pot. Line with moss or a hanging basket liner.

2 Cut a disc of polythene to fit the base of the basket. This stops water from draining through it too quickly.

3 Fill the basket about half full with a mix of two parts ericaceous compost (soil mix) to one of perlite.

4 Cut holes in the side of the liner where trailing plants can be inserted. Push the trailing plants through the holes in the liner. Select the best positions for the remaining plants.

5 Remove the plants from their containers, and fill in the gaps around them with more ericaceous compost (soil mix). Stand the basket on top of a large pot, then water it thoroughly to settle the plants. Leave to drain before hanging it up. With good aftercare, the basket will continue to give considerable pleasure throughout the winter months.

Routine maintenance

Unlike many other garden plants heathers do not need very fertile soil and are adapted to quite harsh conditions. The only additional feed they might require after planting is an annual spring top-dressing of a general fertilizer such as blood, fish and bone. Apply at the rate recommended by the manufacturer, and on no account overfeed. While most garden plants benefit from a dressing of bonemeal in the autumn to encourage good root growth, this is unnecessary, even undesirable for heathers since it tends to turn the soil alkaline.

Keep the heather bed weed free until the plants have formed a weed-suppressing mat, usually after two to three years. A mulch of bark chippings in the autumn or spring, immediately after pruning, is attractive and helps suppress weed seedlings. However, since birds tend to disperse the mulch as they forage for food, check it periodically and cover any bare patches of soil.

A mulch is essential on raised beds that must not be allowed to dry out. Not only does it improve the soil structure, but it prevents moisture from evaporating from the surface. Water all raised beds frequently during the growing season as you would a container.

■ ABOVE
Sprinkle blood, fish and bone around the plants in spring, and fork in lightly.

■ RIGHT
A mulch of bark chippings in the spring or autumn keeps down weeds until the heathers have spread to form a weed-suppressing carpet.

Pruning heathers

1 By late winter, heather flowers will begin to fade and should be removed.

Heathers have few needs once planted. Rigorous pruning is not required. However, if a dwarf cultivar, such as *Calluna* 'Foxii Nana', suddenly produces an uncharacteristic long shoot, it should be cut back immediately to its point of origin. To prevent legginess, in early spring lightly clip over the plants to remove most of the previous year's growth, but do not cut into old wood since this will not produce new stems. Pruning as the new growth emerges gives both summer- and winter-flowering heathers sufficient time to produce enough new wood for good flowering. Pruning individual plants is best done with secateurs, but where the heathers are planted *en masse*, using shears is more practical. Some winter-flowering heathers that are grown mainly for their leaf colour produce flowers that clash with the foliage. The flowering spikes can be removed in mid-winter before they develop fully. Eventually most heathers become straggly and the older plants are best replaced. The tree heath and the somewhat similar *E. australis, E. lusitanica* and *E. × veitchii* have different requirements. They are tall, erect shrubs that should be pruned during the early stages of their development to promote sturdy, bushy growth, and to prevent them from becoming top-heavy. For the first two or three springs after planting reduce the top-growth by a half to two-thirds. In mild climates further pruning is unnecessary, except for removing diseased or dead growth. In areas prone to heavy snowfalls that may damage the plant, cut back the flowered stems by up to a half, after flowering in early summer, to keep the plant compact.

2 In early spring, trim heathers with shears. Cut just below any faded flowers. Avoid cutting into the old wood that will not break away.

3 The appearance will be improved as soon as dead-heading has been done, and as soon as new shoots start to grow the plant will look less manicured.

■ RIGHT
In winter, cut back the developing flowers of heathers that are grown mainly for the interest of their foliage.

RENOVATING A TREE HEATH

1 Tree heaths can become straggly in time but respond well to renovative pruning. This is best spread over two or three years.

2 In early spring, cut back between one-third to a half of all stems to near ground level.

3 The following spring cut back a half or all of the remainder. Any stems left unpruned should be cut hard back the following year.

HEATHERS SHOULD BE PRUNED AS FOLLOWS:

Calluna vulgaris	In late winter, cut back long flowering spikes and trim off spent flowers.
Daboecia cantabrica	In late winter, trim off spent flowers.
Erica carnea	In late spring in alternate years, trim off spent flowers. Cut vigorous cultivars back harder, but only into live wood.
Erica ciliaris *Erica × stuartii*	In early spring, trim off spent flowers.
Erica cinerea *Erica tetralix*	In late winter, trim off dead flowers.
Erica arborea *Erica australis* *Erica erigena* *Erica lusitanica* *Erica terminalis* *Erica × veitchii*	Formative years (1–3): in spring, reduce top growth by a half to two-thirds.
Erica × darleyensis	In late spring to early summer, cut back hard, but only into live wood.
Erica manipuliflora *Erica multiflora* *Erica vagans*	In early spring, trim off spent flowers, cutting back hard but only into live wood.
Erica × watsonii *Erica × williamsii*	In early spring in alternate years, cut back hard, but only into live wood.

4 Old stems pruned hard the previous year should break freely in spring.

Propagation of heathers

Propagate your heathers regularly to ensure that you have good stocks to replace plants as they age and become woody at the base. Various methods are suitable. Since few species are grown, propagation by seed is seldom practised; cultivars can only be increased by vegetative means. All the methods described here are simple and will yield new plants in quantity.

Heather cuttings are less labour-intensive than those of other plants, since they can be overwintered in the rooting medium and need only one potting on for one growing season before being planted out. Where the growing conditions are good, you can even plant them out in their final positions in the first spring, but tighter together than you would larger plants bought from the garden centre. Thin them as they grow.

Layering is a slower method, but the layers need no further attention once the initial procedure is complete. Mound layering and dropping are variations on this technique.

Cuttings

Heather cuttings are best taken around or just after mid-summer. For optimum rooting, include a heel, a small piece of bark from the main stem of the parent plant. The cuttings should be about 2.5–3.5cm (1–1½in) long. If it is not possible to take them with a heel, simply take a cutting of that length from the end of a stem.

The cuttings should have rooted by late summer or early autumn. Overwinter them in a sheltered, shady spot, where the temperature remains fairly even, in the lee of a shrub or wall, for instance. The following spring, either pot them up or transplant them into a nursery bed and grow them on for a season.

TAKING SEMI-RIPE CUTTINGS

1 Fill a seed tray with equal parts of peat and sharp sand. It is not necessary to water the rooting medium at this stage.

2 Select a strong-growing, non-flowering side shoot from the parent plant and grasp it near its point of origin. Pull it sharply away from the main stem, tearing off a tail (heel) of bark from the main stem.

3 Trim the heel with a sharp knife, if necessary.

4 Pinch out the tip of the shoot if it is soft; this also encourages branching once the cutting has rooted.

5 Carefully strip off the foliage from the bottom half of the cutting with finger and thumb (see inset).

6 Immerse the cutting in a copper sulphate solution to kill any bacteria or fungal spores.

7 Dip the base of the cutting in hormone rooting powder and tap off the excess.

8 Insert the cuttings in the dry cuttings medium to half its length using a fine dibber or skewer.

10 Put the cutting in a cool, shady spot outdoors. The bag should fog over. If it dries out, remove the cutting and rewater. Once rooted, remove the bag and overwinter the cutting in the same situation.

9 Water well to seal the compost (potting soil) surface and leave to drain for about 20 minutes. Blow up a polythene bag large enough to hold the tray and seal the tray inside.

Layering

Layering produces fewer plants than cuttings. The advantage is that the new plants remain attached to the parent until rooted, so aftercare is kept to a minimum.

Mound layering is a variation. Both techniques should be used only on plants that have strong stems. Layering and mound layering can be carried out in autumn or spring. The principle is to bring the stems into contact with soil and so encourage rooting at that point. The stems of most other shrubs need wounding to encourage root production, but this is not so with heathers.

Roots should have formed by the following autumn, after which the rooted stems can be severed from the parent and grown on.

LAYERING

1 Dig a shallow trench in autumn and spring around the perimeter of the plant.

2 Mix the excavated soil with sharp sand and peat or garden compost to make a friable mixture.

3 Spread out the outer stems of the heather and sprinkle in the soil mixture.

4 Hold the stems in place with wires bent into a U shape. The layers will take about a year to root, after which they can be severed from the parent plant and either potted up or planted out.

MOUND LAYERING

1 Prepare a sandy, friable mixture of garden soil, sand, and peat or garden compost. Mound this around the stems of the plant, spreading them apart with your fingers if necessary.

2 Cover the stems to within about 2.5–5cm (1–2in) of their tips. Keep the mound well watered during dry spells in the summer. You may need to replenish the mound if heavy rainfall washes away some of the soil. The shoots should have rooted by late summer, when they can be separated from the parent plant and potted up or planted out.

Dropping

Heathers that have been allowed to become woody at the base are best increased by dropping.

Dropping is best practised in the dormant season since it involves lifting the plant – a procedure that normally checks growth. To keep disturbance to a minimum, take care not to damage the root system when lifting the plant.

The stems should have formed roots by the following autumn, when they can be detached from the parent plant and then grown on.

1 Lift the entire plant in the dormant season. Keep rootball disturbance to a minimum.

2 Cut back any straggly or congested stems.

3 Dig a large hole that will accommodate the plant, and allow you to bury it, so that only the top 2.5–5cm (1–2in) of stem remains above soil level.

4 Mix the excavated soil with sand and peat or garden compost and work it around the plant. Each stem should be in contact with the soil and not touch its neighbours. The shoots should develop roots by the following autumn. Sever them from the parent plant and either pot up or plant out.

Heathers for indoor decoration

Heathers can be used for indoor flower decorations, cut or dried, or as pot plants. Since heather colours are usually subtle, the best effects are realized using a restricted palette of dusky pinks, deep reds and purples, while strong clear blues and yellows are best avoided.

Tender heathers are available as pot plants in garden centres, florists and supermarkets from the autumn onwards. They can be arranged in containers with other pot plants (that have a similar colour range), winter-flowering pansies or miniature roses. Hardy heathers are equally suitable companions.

You could also add dried gourds or fresh fruits such as pomegranates, apples or clementines, or even vegetables. White or purple aubergines or globe artichokes are very effective. Fill in any gaps in the arrangement with moss.

When the arrangement is past its peak, any hardy heathers with the other hardy plants, can be planted out in the garden. To keep the arrangement fresh, spray it period-ically with distilled water. Remove the moss periodically and check that the individual pots are not drying out. Water sparingly, if necessary, and replace the moss. Such an

MAKING AN ARRANGEMENT WITH HEATHERS IN POTS

1 Line the container, unless solid-based, with polythene to prevent water from leaking out.

2 Select the best positions for the plants. Stand the pots on pieces of crumpled aluminium foil if they need raising.

3 Fill in any gaps in the arrangement with moss.

arrangement, if properly cared for, will give pleasure for several weeks. Heathers are available from florists as cut flowers usually from the autumn to spring. If you want to use material from your own plants, cut it in the early morning, when the heathers are

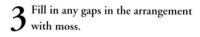

HEATHERS IN INDOOR DECORATION

Hardy heathers suitable for cutting

Calluna vulgaris
'Alexandra'
'Annemarie'
'Anthony Davis'
'Elsie Purnell'
'H.E. Beale'
'Mair's Variety'
'My Dream'
'Peter Sparkes'
Erica vagans 'Viridiflora'

DRYING HEATHERS USING SILICA GEL

1 Put down a 1cm (½in) layer of a drying agent, such as silica gel, in a lidded plastic container. Lay the stems on the gel, making sure that they do not touch, then sprinkle more gel over them.

2 Cover the container and seal the lid with tape. The stems should be dry within 3–6 days. Carefully shake them free of gel. You can lengthen the stems by wiring them with florist's stub wire bent into U shapes.

at their freshest and the stems turgid after the dew. Cut the stems as long as possible but without cutting into the old wood that will not regenerate, unless you are taking material from one of the tree heaths.

Condition the stems by standing them in distilled water, as deep as possible, for at least an hour before arranging. Revive and straighten wilted blooms by wrapping them in paper and then stand them in tepid water to which cut flower food has been added. Heather flowers can be arranged in water or florist's foam (oasis). To keep arrangements in

florist's foam fresh, spray periodically with tepid distilled water.

For more long-lasting arrangements heather flowers can be dried. There are no hard and fast rules for drying plant material, but for the best colour retention, dry as soon as possible after picking.

To air-dry heathers, tie around five or six stems in loose bunches, spiralling them to ensure good air circulation. Hang them upside down in a warm, dry, well-ventilated place. The drying process takes about 7–10 days. For a quicker but more expensive method use silica gel.

WIRING A HEATHER STEM

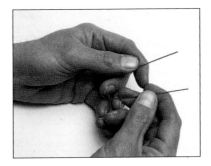

1 Bend a florist's stub wire into a U shape.

2 Hold the wire parallel with the heather stem, the bend facing towards the tip. Twist one leg of the U around the other a couple of times to hold the stem firmly.

3 Trim the wire to the desired length with scissors or secateurs.

Heather problems

Heathers are remarkably free of pests and diseases if they are growing strongly in a habitat that suits them. Gardeners in rural areas can experience trouble from rabbits, hares and deer that graze on the plants, the young growth being particularly tasty. The most effective and humane method of control is to erect a barrier to keep the pests out of the garden. To deter rabbits and hares this should be sunk about 30–45cm (12–18in) into the ground, and it should be 90cm (3ft) high. A height of 2m (6ft) is necessary to keep deer out.

Heathers are also susceptible to various soil-borne fungal diseases. Botrytis mainly affects *Calluna* and affects the growing tips, which die back. Rhizoctonia mainly affects *Calluna* but here browning of the foliage takes place from ground level upwards, usually reaching a few centimetres from the ground. Pythium tends to attack specific stems on both *Calluna* and *Erica*. One of the characteristic symptoms is a reddening of the foliage. In severe cases the plant can be killed. Phytophthora is a killer that fortunately is not that common. It attacks in a similar way to Rhizoctonia, often spreading from one point. Fortunately, most fungal problems occur if the heathers are growing in containers, as all of these pathogens require high soil temperatures and moist conditions. Garden soil rarely reaches the critical temperatures.

Where only part of the plant is affected, trim off the damaged foliage and then boost the plant with a foliar feed to promote recovery – some are specially formulated for sickening plants. If the whole plant is affected, dig it up and burn it. You will need to replace the soil with fresh soil from another part of the garden before replanting.

This is a good opportunity for taking preventive measures if the problem is severe. If the soil is prone to dampness, improve the drainage either by laying land drains or by digging in coarse grit or organic matter (see Cultivation). If the soil is permanently wet because of a high water-table, either move your heathers elsewhere, or make a raised bed for them.

Botrytis attacks the growing tips, which wilt and die back.

Pythium tends to attack specific stems and is normally characterized by a reddening of the foliage. The plant on the left is under attack and has been placed alongside a healthy plant. In severe cases pythium kills the plant.

Rhizoctonia, like botrytis, tends to attack *Calluna*. Here the symptoms are a general browning of the lower foliage, often in an even manner for about 2.5cm (1in) above the soil. Attacks of rhizoctonia often kill the plant.

Calendar

Spring

Plant new stock. Mulch newly-planted heather beds and raised beds with bark chippings. Top-dress heathers grown in heather beds with blood, fish and bone. Top-dress containers with blood, fish and bone; water in sequestered iron (iron chelate). Plant out or pot up flagging heathers that have been grown for winter interest in containers or hanging baskets. Prune – either clip over with shears or secateurs or, in the case of tall heathers, cut back by a half to two-thirds (the first two seasons after planting only). Renovate overgrown or straggly tall heathers. Increase your stock by mound layering. Plant out cuttings taken the previous summer.

Dead-head winter-flowering heathers in spring.

Summer

Plant new stock, except during periods of prolonged drought. Mulch newly-planted heather beds and raised beds with bark chippings. Water heathers in containers and raised beds regularly with soft water. Place outdoors tender heathers grown under glass. In cold districts cut back the flowered stems on tall-growing heathers to keep them compact enough to withstand possible damage from winter snow. Take cuttings to increase your stock (using a heated propagator for early cuttings and those taken from tender heathers). Water plants being propagated by mound layering during periods of drought. Replenish the mound if heavy rainfall washes away soil. Sever the rooted stems from the parent plant if propagating in spring by mound layering.

Autumn

Plant new stock. Mulch newly-planted heather beds and raised beds with bark chippings. Place tender, container-grown heathers indoors again before the first frosts if they have been stood outside over summer. Take heeled cuttings, or layer plants to increase your stock. Plant out cuttings taken the previous autumn. Sever rooted stems from the parent plant where layered the previous autumn. Lift any plants propagated by dropping the previous winter, and sever newly-rooted stems from the parent.

Winter

Plant new stock, except when the ground is frozen or waterlogged. Mulch newly-planted heather beds and raised beds with bark chippings. Plant up new containers, window boxes and hanging baskets for winter interest. Loosely cover heathers in containers outdoors with dry straw or bracken, held in place with chicken wire. Bring heathers in hanging baskets under cover during severe cold weather. Remove the developing flowers of heathers grown primarily for their foliage effect. Ventilate heathers grown under glass whenever the temperature rises above 5 °C (41 °F). Increase your stock by dropping.

Increase your stock of heathers by layering in autumn.

Other recommended heathers

Approximate heights and spreads are given at the end of each description, the first figure indicating the height.

Calluna vulgaris 'Annemarie'. Bell-shaped, double, rose-pink flowers from mid-summer to late autumn. 50cm (20in) x 60cm (24in).

Calluna vulgaris 'Alexandra', 'Alicia' and Anette'.

Calluna vulgaris 'Anthony Davis'. White flowers in late summer; grey-green foliage. 45cm (18in) x 50cm (20in).

Calluna vulgaris 'Beoley Gold'. Bright golden yellow foliage and bell-shaped, white flowers in late summer. 35cm (14in) x 60cm (24in).

Calluna vulgaris 'County Wicklow'. Bell-shaped, double, pale pink flowers from mid- to late summer. 25cm (10in) x 35cm (14in).

Calluna vulgaris 'Elsie Purnell'. Greyish-green foliage; bell-shaped, double, pale pink flowers from mid- to late summer. 40cm (16in) x 75cm (30in).

Calluna vulgaris 'Foxii Nana'. Bell-shaped, mauve flowers in late summer. 15cm (6in) x 30cm (12in).

Calluna vulgaris 'H.E. Beale' (syn. *C. v.* 'Pink Beale'). Bell-shaped, double, mid-pink flowers from mid- to late summer. 60cm (24in) x 60cm (24in).

Calluna vulgaris 'Hammondii'. Bell-shaped, white flowers in late summer. 75cm (30in) x 75cm (30in).

Calluna vulgaris 'J.H. Hamilton'. Double, dark pink flowers from mid- to late summer. 10cm (4in) x 25cm (10in).

Calluna vulgaris 'Joy Vanstone'. Yellow-gold foliage turning orange in winter; bell-shaped, pink flowers in late summer. 50cm (20in) x 60cm (24in).

Calluna vulgaris 'Kerstin'. Greyish-lilac leaves, the new growth tipped with light yellow and red in spring; bell-shaped, mauve flowers from mid-summer through to late autumn. 50cm (20in) x 45cm (18in).

Calluna vulgaris 'Kinlochruel'. Double, white flowers from mid- to late summer. 25cm (10in) x 40cm (16in).

Calluna vulgaris 'Mair's Variety' (syn. *C. v.* 'Elongata'). Bell-shaped, white flowers in late summer. 40cm (16in) x 60cm (24in).

Calluna vulgaris 'Mullion'. Lilac-pink flowers in late summer; dark green foliage. 20cm (8in) x 50cm (20in).

Calluna vulgaris 'Multicolor'. Copper foliage flecked with orange and red all year; bell-shaped, mauve flowers from mid-summer to late autumn. 10cm (4in) x 25cm (10in).

Calluna vulgaris 'Orange Queen'. Golden yellow foliage turning bronze in autumn, and orange in winter; lavender flowers from late summer to mid-autumn. 30cm (12in) x 50cm (20in).

Calluna vulgaris 'Peter Sparkes'. Double, pink flowers from mid-summer to late autumn. 25cm (10in) x 55cm (22in).

Calluna vulgaris 'Red Carpet' (syn. *C. v.* 'Marinka'). Golden-yellow foliage that reddens after hard frosts in winter; bell-shaped, mauve-pink flowers from mid-summer to late autumn. 20cm (8in) x 45cm (18in).

Calluna vulgaris 'Red Favorit' Double crimson flowers in late summer; dark green foliage. 20cm (8in) x 70cm (28in).

Calluna vulgaris 'Red Pimpernel'. Crimson flowers from late summer to autumn.

Calluna vulgaris 'Red Pimpernel'.

20cm (8in) x 45cm (18in).

Calluna vulgaris 'Red Star'. Double deep lilac-pink flowers from late summer to mid-autumn; dark green foliage. 40cm (16in) x 60cm (24in).

Calluna vulgaris 'Robert Chapman'. Golden-yellow foliage in summer turning orange in autumn, and red in winter and spring; lavender flowers from late summer to mid-autumn. 25cm (10in) x 65cm (26in).

Calluna vulgaris 'Roland Haagen'. Golden yellow foliage turning bright orange with darker tips in winter; mauve yellow flowers in late summer. 15cm (6in) x 35cm (14in).

Calluna vulgaris 'Serlei Aurea'. Yellowish-green foliage tipped with yellow in summer and autumn; bell-shaped, white flowers in late summer. 50cm (20in) x 40cm (16in).

Calluna vulgaris 'Silver
Queen'. Silver-grey foliage;
bell-shaped, pale mauve
flowers from mid- to late
summer. 40cm (16in) x
55cm (22in).

Calluna vulgaris 'Silver Rose'.
Lilac-pink flowers in late
summer ; silver-grey, hairy
foliage. 40cm (16in) x
50cm (20in).

Calluna vulgaris 'Sir John
Charrington'. Golden yellow
leaves in summer that deepen
to orange and red in winter;
bell-shaped, mauve-pink
flowers in autumn. 40cm
(16in) x 60cm (24in).

Calluna vulgaris 'Sister Anne'.
Grey-green foliage turning
bronze in winter; bell-shaped,
mauve flowers in late summer.
10cm (4in) x 25cm (10in).

Calluna vulgaris 'Spring
Cream'. Mid-green foliage
tipped cream in spring, yellow
in autumn and winter; white
flowers from late summer to
late autumn. 35cm (14in) x
45cm (18in).

Calluna vulgaris 'Spring
Torch' (syn. *C. v.* 'Spring
Charm'). Foliage tipped with
cream, orange and red in
spring; bell-shaped, mauve
flowers from mid-summer to
late autumn. 40cm (16in)x
60cm (24in).

Calluna vulgaris 'Sunset'.
Golden-yellow foliage in
summer turning red in
autumn and winter, and

Calluna vulgaris 'White
Coral'.

lilac-pink flowers from late
summer to mid-autumn.
20cm (8in) x 45cm (18in).

Calluna vulgaris 'White
Coral'. White flowers from
mid-summer to late autumn.
30cm (12in) x 40cm (16in).

Calluna vulgaris 'White
Lawn'. Bell-shaped, white
flowers in late summer. 5cm
(2in) x 40cm (16in).

Daboecia cantabrica
'Bicolor'. Urn-shaped, white,
pink and purple flowers (some
streaked) in mid- to late
summer. 25cm (10in) x
65cm (26in).

Daboecia cantabrica
'Hookstone Purple'. Urn-
shaped, purple flowers in mid-
to late summer. 25cm (10in) x
65cm (26in).

Daboecia cantabrica
'Rainbow'. Urn-shaped, deep-
purple flowers from mid- to
late summer; the foliage is
variegated with red and

yellow. 25cm (10in) x 65cm
(26in).

Daboecia× scotica
'Silverwells'. Urn-shaped,
white flowers in summer.
15cm (6in) x 35cm (14in).

Daboecia× scotica 'William
Buchanan'. Urn-shaped,
purplish-crimson flowers in
mid- to late summer. 35cm
(14in) x 55cm (22in).

Erica arborea 'Albert's Gold'.
Yellow foliage all year,
brightest colour in winter and
spring; sparse, lightly scented
flowers in spring. 2m (6ft) x
80cm (32in).

Erica australis (Spanish
heath). Purplish-pink flowers
from mid-spring to early
summer. 2m (6ft) x 1m (3ft).
'Mr Robert' has white flowers
and light green foliage. 1.8m
(64in) x 85cm (34in).

Erica canaliculata
(Channelled heath). Pale pink
to near white flowers from
winter to early spring. 2m (6ft)

Daboecia cantabrica
'Rainbow'.

x 1.2m (4ft). Not hardy.

Erica carnea 'Adrienne
Duncan'. Lilac-pink flowers
from mid-winter to mid-
spring; dark green foliage
tinged bronze. 15cm (6in) x
35cm (14in).

Erica carnea 'Ann Sparkes'.
Rose-pink flowers darkening
to lilac-pink from late winter
to late spring; orange foliage
tipped bronze turning crimson
in winter. 15cm (6in) x
25cm (10in).

Erica carnea 'Challenger' .
Flowers with magenta corollas
and crimson sepals from mid-
winter to mid-spring; dark
green foliage. 15cm (6in) x
45cm (18in).

Erica carnea 'Foxhollow
Fairy'. "Bicolor" flowers with
near-white corollas and pink
calyces, the whole flower
ageing pink. 15cm (6in) x
45cm (18in).

Erica carnea 'Golden Starlet'.
Glowing yellow foliage,
turning lime green in winter;
white flowers from mid-winter
to early spring. 15cm (6in) x
40cm (16in).

Erica carnea 'Myretoun
Ruby'. Lilac pink flowers,
deepening through magenta to
crimson from mid-winter to
spring. 15cm (6in) x 45cm
(18in).

Erica carnea 'Springwood
White'. Abundant white
flowers from mid-winter to
late spring. 15cm (67in) x

Erica cinerea 'Autumn Pink'.'

45cm (18in).
Erica carnea 'Westwood Yellow'. Yellow foliage throughout the year; shell-pink flowers darkening to lilac-pink. 15cm (6in) x 30cm (12in).
Erica ciliaris 'David McClintock'. Bicolor flowers with white bases and purplish-pink mouths from mid-summer to autumn. 30cm (12in) x 45cm (18in).
Erica cinerea 'Autumn Pink'. Urn-shaped, pink flowers during autumn. 30cm (12in) x 45cm (18in).
Erica cinerea 'Blossom Time'. Urn-shaped, magenta flowers in mid- to late summer. 30cm (12in) x 55cm (22in)
Erica cinerea 'Champs Hill'. Urn-shaped, dusky rose-pink flowers in mid- to late summer. 35cm (14in) x 45cm (18in).
Erica cinerea 'Eden Valley'. Urn-shaped, lavender-pink

flowers with white bases in mid- to late summer. 20cm (8in) x 50cm (20in).
Erica cinerea 'Golden Hue'. Pale yellow foliage tipped orange in winter; amethyst flowers from mid-summer to autumn. 35cm (14in) x 70cm (28in).
Erica cinerea 'Hookstone White'. White flowers from mid-summer to autumn. 35cm (14in) x 65cm (26in).
Erica cinerea 'Lady Skelton'. Urn-shaped, ruby flowers in mid- to late summer. 10cm (4in) x 15cm (6in).
Erica cinerea 'Pentreath'. Urn-shaped, beetroot-red flowers in mid- to late summer. 30cm (12in) x 60cm (24in).

Erica cinerea 'Blossom Time'.

Erica cinerea 'Pink Ice' (syn. *E. c.* 'Pink Lace'). Foliage tinged bronze when young and in winter; urn-shaped, rose-pink flowers in mid- to late

Erica cinerea 'Champs Hill'.

summer. 20cm (8in) x 35cm (14in).
Erica cinerea 'Stephen Davis'. Luminous red, urn-shaped flowers in mid- to late summer. 25cm (10in) x 45cm (18in).
Erica mackaiana 'Shining Light'. White flowers from mid-summer to autumn; grey-green foliage. 25cm (10in) x 55cm (22in).
Erica terminalis (syn. *E. corsica* , *E. stricta*; Corsican heath). Lilac-pink flowers from mid-summer to early autumn. 1m (3ft) x 1m (3ft).
Erica tetralix 'Alba Mollis'. Grey-green foliage tipped silver-grey; white flowers from early summer to autumn. 20cm (8in) x 30cm (12in).
Erica tetralix 'Con Underwood'. Magenta flower from mid-summer to late autumn; grey-green foliage. 25cm (10in) x 35cm (14in).
Erica tetralix 'Pink Star'.

Lilac-pink flowers from mid-summer to early autumn; grey-green foliage. 20cm (8in) x 35cm (14in).
Erica vagans 'Kevernensis Alba'. Cylindrical to bell-shaped, white flowers in late summer. 30cm (12in) x 50cm (20in).
Erica vagans 'Lyonesse'. White flowers from late summer to autumn. 25cm (10in) x 50cm (20in).
Erica vagans 'Mrs D.F. Maxwell'. Deep rose pink flowers from late summer to autumn; dark green foliage. 30cm (12in) x 45cm (18in).
Erica vagans 'St Keverne'.

Erica cinerea 'Lady's Skeleton'.

Bell-shaped, bright pink flowers in late summer. 30cm (12in) x 50cm (20in).
Erica 'Valerie Griffiths'. Yellow leaves, deepening to darker yellow in autumn; bell-shaped, pale pink flowers from early summer through to mid-summer. 40cm (16in) x 55cm (22in).

Index

Abies concolor 'Compacta', 16
A. lasiocarpa var. *arizonica*
  'Compacta', 16
acid soils, 41
Andromeda polifolia, 13
Arctostaphylos uva-ursi, 13

Berberis temolaica, 14
Buxus sempervivens, 16
buying heathers, 40

Calluna, 8–9, 12, 18–19, 41, 58
  C. vagans 'Viridiflora', 56
  C. vulgaris, 9, 14, 15, 18,
    20–3, 51
    C. v. 'Alba Rigida', 20
    C. v. 'Alexandra', 46, 56, 60
    C. v. 'Alicia', 46, 60
    C. v. 'Alison Yates', 20
    C. v. 'Annemarie', 56, 60
    C. v. 'Anette', 46, 60
    C. v. 'Anthony Davis', 56
    C. v. 'Arran Gold', 21
    C. v. 'Beoley Gold', 14, 17,
      18, 60
    C. v. 'County Wicklow', 60
    C. v. 'Cuprea', 14
    C. v. 'Dark Beauty', 21
    C. v. 'Darkness', 19, 21
    C. v. 'Elongata', 60
    C. v. 'Elsie Purnell', 56, 60
    C. v. 'Firefly', 22
    C. v. 'Foxii Nana', 50, 60
    C. v. 'Golden Carpet', 46
    C. v. 'Golden Feather', 17
    C. v. 'Hammondii', 60
    C. v. 'Hammondii
      Aureifolia', 22
    C. v. 'H.E. Beale', 56, 60
    C. v. 'J.H. Hamilton', 60
    C. v. 'Joy Vanstone', 60
    C. v. 'Kerstin', 60
    C. v. 'Kinlochruel', 60
    C. v. 'Mair's Variety', 56, 60
    C. v. 'Marinka', 60
    C. v. 'Mullion', 60
    C. v. 'Multicolor', 17, 60
    C. v. 'My Dream', 23, 56

    C. v. 'Orange Queen', 60
    C. v. 'Peter Sparkes', 56, 60
    C. v. 'Pink Beale', 60
    C. v. 'Red Carpet', 17, 60
    C. v. 'Red Favorit', 60
    C. v. 'Red Fred', 17
    C. v. 'Red Pimpernel', 60
    C. v. 'Red Star', 60
    C. v. 'Robert Chapman',
      14, 17, 60
    C. v. 'Roland Haagen', 17
    C. v. 'Serlei Aurea', 17, 60
    C. v. 'Silver Queen', 61
    C. v. 'Silver Rose', 61
    C. v. 'Sir John Charrington',
      17, 61
    C. v. 'Sister Anne', 17, 61
    C. v. 'Snowball', 23
    C. v. 'Spring Cream', 17
    C. v. 'Spring Torch', 61
    C. v. 'Sunset', 17, 61
    C. v. 'Tib', 23, 46, 61
    C. v. 'White Coral', 61
    C. v. 'White Lawn', 61
    C. v. 'Wickwar Flame', 17,
      18, 23
Chamaecyparis obtusa 'Nana
  Aurea', 16
  C. pisifera 'Filifera Aurea', 16

conifers, 13–14, 16
containers, growing heathers
  in, 46–7
Cornus alba 'Sibirica', 14
  C. sanguinea 'Winter Beauty', 14
  C. stolonifera 'Flaviramea', 14
cultivation, 41–9
cut flowers, 56–7
cuttings, 52–3
Cytisus scoparius, 13

Daboecia, 8–9, 18, 41
  D. azorica, 18
  D. cantabrica, 18, 51
    D. c. 'Alba', 24
    D. c. 'Atropurpurea', 24
    D. c. 'Bicolor', 61
    D. c. 'Hookstone Purple', 61
    D. c. 'Rainbow', 61
    D. c. 'Whalley', 46
    D. c. 'Waley's Red', 25
  D. × *scotica*, 18
    D. × scotica 'Silverwells', 61
    D. × scotica 'William
      Buchanan', 61
dead-heading, 50
diseases, 58
dropping, 54, 55
drying heathers, 57

Erica, 8,–9, 12, 18–19, 41, 43,
  58
  E. arborea, 9, 19, 51
    E. a. 'Albert's Gold', 61
  E. australis, 19, 50, 51, 61
    E. a. 'Mr Robert', 61
    E .a. 'Riverslea', 25
  E. canaliculata, 19, 43, 61
  E. carnea, 18, 19, 26–8, 41, 51
    E. c. 'Adrienne Duncan',
      14, 61
    E. c. 'Alexandra', 46
    E. c. 'Alicia', 46
    E. c. 'Anette', 46
    E. c. 'Ann Sparkes', 17, 61
    E. c. 'Aurea', 26
    E. c. 'Barry Sellers', 17
    E. c. 'Challenger', 61
    E. c. 'Eileen Porter', 26
    E. c. 'Foxhollow', 17, 19, 61
    E. c. 'Golden Starlet', 17, 61
    E. c. 'January Sun', 46
    E. c. 'King George', 27
    E. c. 'Myretoun Ruby', 27,
      35, 61
    E. c. 'Praecox Rubra', 27
    E. c. 'Rosy Gem', 28
    E. c. 'Springwood White',
      12, 28, 46, 61
    E. c. 'Urville', 28
    E. c. 'Vivellii', 14, 28
    E. c. 'Westwood Yellow', 17
  E. ciliaris, 51
  E. cinerea, 9, 15, 19, 29–33, 51
    E. c. 'Alfred Bowerman', 29
    E. c. 'Autumn Pink', 62
    E. c. 'Blossom Time', 62
    E. c. 'C.D. Eason', 29
    E. c. 'C.G. Best', 30
    E. c. 'Champs Hill', 62
    E. c. 'Eden Valley', 62
    E. c. 'Fiddler's Gold', 17, 30
    E .c. 'Golden Drop', 30
    E. c. 'Golden Hue', 17, 62
    E. c. 'Golden Sport', 31
    E. c. 'Heidebrand', 31
    E. c. 'Hookstone White', 62
    E. c. 'Lady Skelton', 62

E. c. 'Lime Soda', 17
E. c. 'Pentreath', 32, 33, 62
E. c. 'Pink Ice', 62
E. c. 'P.S. Patrick', 31
E. c. 'Rock Pool', 17
E. c. 'Snow Cream', 32
E. c. 'Stephen Davis', 62
E. c. 'Summer Gold', 33
E. c. 'Velvet Night', 33
E. c. 'Windlebrooke', 17
E. corsica, 62
E. × darleyensis, 9, 14, 18, 19, 34–5, 41, 51
E. × darleyensis 'Archie Graham', 34
E. × darleyensis 'Arthur Johnson', 34
E. × darleyensis 'Jack H. Brummage', 34
E. × darleyensis 'Jenny Porter', 17
E. × darleyensis 'J.W. Porter', 17
E. × darleyensis 'Kramers Röte', 35
E. × darleyensis 'Margaret Porter', 15
E. × darleyensis 'Silberschmelze', 35
E. × darleyensis 'White Perfection', 35
E. erigena, 9, 36, 41, 51
E. e. 'Brian Proudley', 36

E. e. 'Golden Lady', 17
E. gracilis, 43
E. hiemalis, 43
E. lusitanica, 14, 20, 50, 51
E. l. 'George Hunt', 36
E. mackaiana, 19
E. m. 'Shining Light', 62
E. manipuliflora, 41, 51
E. m. ssp. *E. vagans*, 37
E. multiflora, 51
E. stricta, 62
E. × stuartii, 19, 51
E. × stuartii 'Irish Lemon', 37
E. terminalis, 41, 51, 62
E. t. 'Alba Mollis', 62
E. t. 'Con Underwood', 62
E. tetralix, 51
E. vagans, 15, 19, 38–9, 41, 51
E. v. 'Birch Glow', 38
E. v. 'Hookstone Rosea', 38
E. v. 'Kevernensis Alba', 62
E. v. 'Lyonesse', 62
E. v. 'Mrs D. F. Maxwell', 62
E. v. 'Pink Star', 62
E. v. 'St Keverne', 62
E. v. 'Summertime', 38
E. v. 'Valerie Proudley', 17, 39
E. v. 'Viridiflora', 39, 56
E. 'Valerie Griffiths', 62
E. × veitchii, 50, 51
E. × watsonii, 51
E. × williamsii, 19, 41, 51

E. × williamsii 'P.D. Williams', 39
fertilizers, 46–7, 49
flowers of sulphur, 44, 45

fungal diseases, 58

hanging baskets, 48

indoor decorations, 56–7

Juniperus communis 'Hibernica', 13, 16
J. × media 'Pfitzeriana', 16
J. × media 'Plumosa Aurea', 16
J. procumbens 'Nana', 16
J. squamata 'Blue Star', 13, 16
J. s. 'Holger', 16
J. virginiana 'Grey Owl', 16

layering, 52, 54

Mahonia × media 'Charity', 14
Microbiota decussata, 16
mound layering, 54
mulches, 49

pests, 58
pH scale, soil acidity, 41
Picea glauca var. *albertiana* 'Conica', 16
P. mariana 'Nana', 16
Pinus heldreichii var.

leucodermis 'Schmidtii', 16
planting, 42, 46–7
propagation, 52–5
pruning, 50–1
Prunus subhirtella 'Autumnalis', 14

raised beds, 44–5, 49
renovating old plants, 51
Rhododendron impeditum, 13
Rubus thibetanus, 14

Salix. alba var. *vitellina* 'Britzensis', 14
S. irrorata, 14
soil, 41, 44–5, 58

tender heathers, 43
Thuja orientalis 'Aurea Nana', 13, 16
T. plicata 'Stoneham Gold', 13, 16
Tree heath, 9, 13, 19, 50

Ulex europaeus, 13, 15

Vaccinium vitis-idaea, 13
Viburnum × bodnantense 'Dawn', 14
V. tinus, 14

watering, 44–5, 47, 49
wiring heather stems, 57

ACKNOWLEDGEMENTS

The publishers would like to thank the Heather Society, Denbeigh, All Saints Road, Creeting St. Mary, Ipswich IP6 8PJ for all the information they supplied, and Mrs Mary Bowerman and Mr and Mrs A. Keech for allowing photography of their gardens. They would also like to thank the following for the loan of pictures: The Harpur Garden Picture Library, pages 6–7 (R.H.S. Wisley), 11 and 13 (Adrian Bloom); Harry Smith, pages 10, 12, 14, 15t, 15b, 16b, 43, 63 and 64; The Garden Picture Library, pages 16t (© John Glover), 17 (© Brigitte Thomas), and 45 (© Lynne Brotche); Peter McHoy, pages 8, 25, 26t, 27t, 27m, 28t, 29br, 35t and 37b; Photos Horticultural, pages 30tl, 31b, 32 and 37b; David Small, pages 58l, 58m and 58r and the British Heather Grower's Association, pages 29b and 33.